# DOCTOR AT STONE CREEK

## Tony Fouracre

Highgate Publications (Beverley) Ltd
1993

British Library Cataloguing in Publication Data Available

© 1993 Anthony Fouracre

ISBN 0 948929 81 2

Published by
Highgate Publications (Beverley) Ltd.
24 Wylies Road, Beverley, HU17 7AP
Telephone (0482) 866826

Produced by
B. A. Print
4 Newbegin, Lairgate, Beverley, HU17 8EG
Telephone (0482) 886017

*Cover Picture:* Cracker *setting out for Holland: the start of the North Sea Race, 9 July 1988.*
*(Reproduced by courtesy* Hull Daily Mail*) .*

# Preface

Do seasiders have the sea in their veins?

My first boat in 1937 was a contraption of wood, canvas and Meccano, waterproofed with tar from the gasworks. In this I used to alarm my mother by going too far out to sea.

When I returned to Withernsea in the fifties it seemed natural to acquire a boat, although both money and boats were in short supply. In partnership with a local baker, Bill Watts, I bought a Prout folding sailing dinghy for £40. We called her *Pourquoi* – a pun on our surnames – and we practised the skills of launching and landing from an open beach and setting and hauling long lines and crab pots. We learned that in the open sea a small black buoy is more visible than a white one.

The natural progression of boating enthusiasts is towards something larger and in 1957 we obtained from Kenneth Gibbs on the Thames an 18-foot centreboard sloop with two canvas berths. We called her *Pourquoi Pas,* which was a little pretentious since there was a famous cruising yacht of that name.

In those days there were not many pleasure craft on the Humber. At Stone Creek we joined a select company of squatters who, when threatened with eviction, overnight formed the Stone Creek Boat Club, and our secretary, Brian Nordon, a lawyer, negotiated a lease with the riparian owners, the Crown Estates, who managed adjacent Sunk Island. Our doyen and first captain was Vin Lockey, a well-known Withernsea character. Former aviator and motor engineer, he was never at a loss with any of our mechanical problems, often solving them in original and unorthodox ways like putting diesel in a petrol engine to free a sticking valve.

All my yachts – four – have been berthed at Stone Creek, a quiet backwater opposite Immingham. Very much do-it-yourself, we cast concrete mooring blocks in old tyres, and once I used the top of an Aga cooker as a sinker.

For 22 years I thought Stone Creek was idyllic. I never tired of watching the tide cover the mudflats faster than a man can walk, and then creep slowly up the bank or, if there was a southerly gale, break over the top. Nor of a gentle evening sail when, to quote Langstone Hughes:

> 'I have seen the River's muddy bosom
> Turn all golden in the sunset.'

The Humber is not the easiest of rivers. With tides second in intensity only to the Severn, it should be treated with respect. Six knots of tide with you helps you scoot over the ground; against, and you are sailing backwards. Should you run aground on full ebb or flood, the situation is immediately fraught. Several trawlers have been rolled over and lost, one within sight of the Hull fish dock gates.

But in *Pourquoi Pas* and my next boat, a Debutante, I explored the river from Spurn to Grimsby in the east to Apex point in the west, the Trent up to West Stockwith, and the Ouse to Nun Monkton above York. We have visited all the tidal creeks: Killingholme and East Halton Skitter in the lower Humber and, above Hull, Barrow, Barton, Hessle, Brough and Wintringham Havens. A favourite destination was South Ferriby Sluice and the peaceful River Ancholme. It still is, but now I take my grandchildren.

My wife, who does not care for boating, has been indulgent of my passion. She was extremely trusting about my taking the children. I remember Paul aged six sleeping alone in his tent (except for his teddy) on the bank of the River Ancholme at Brandy Wharf. He could already swim, of course.

In 1970 with money left me by an aunt I bought a Hurley 22 so we called her *Mianti*. She had pretty lines and was a good sea boat. Passages further afield were now possible. After sailing to Harwich with my sons Robert and Paul, the following year Paul and I, accompanied by David Suddaby, made our first passage to Holland.

Whilst the North Sea is well supplied with sea marks – buoys, lightships and gas platforms – one can still sail all day without encountering any of them. From the Leman gasfield to Ijmuiden is 80 miles, from the Indefatigable rigs to Den Helder is 90 miles, and our average sped is four knots.

For our first two crossings we relied on dead reckoning. What can be more satisfying than making a landfall where you hope to be after sailing a compass course and making due allowance for leeway, boat speed and tidal streams which vary hour by hour?

The classic advice is to make a dawn landfall when the shoreline becomes visible and the lights can still be identified. I have only managed this once, at Den Helder, where the light is seen at 30 miles and also at Spurn, but, sadly for yachtsmen, Spurn light has now been extinguished. Cromer light has a range of 23 miles. This is helpful on a passage from Spurn to the south of Holland since, after 60 miles at sea, you close the north Norfolk coast.

In 1979 I had the chance to buy a Westerly Centaur. This has proved to be my ideal boat and I have no intentions of changing her. Small enough to maintain myself and sail single-handed, yet she is large enough to be stable and a safe sea boat. She belonged to a local chicken farmer, John Biglin. His wife told me they called her *Cracker* because she was paid for out of the sales of cracked eggs. Well, for me she is a 'cracker' in every respect. Together we have crossed the North Sea 12 times and cruised the Waddenzee, the Ijsselmeer and the East and West Schelde.

In 1983 I moved *Cracker* to the new Hull Marina. Whilst I miss the solitude of Stone Creek, the Marina is more convenient, easier for boarding, and gives longer time of access to the river.

This book would be incomplete unless I mentioned my trio of stalwart sailing companions, Trevor Dalby, Tony Johnson and Brian Nordon, with whom I have spent many happy hours on the Humber and the North Sea.

When I was a wakeful child my father would soothe me to sleep by encouraging me to 'blow out the lighthouse light'. I was only successful in this on his command, as he knew the sequence of flashes: two shorts and a long – Morse code for 'U', which warns shipping:

'You are running into danger.'

Like Spurn, Withernsea light is no longer lit, but any profit from this booklet about the sailing experiences which have given me so much pleasure will go to our Lighthouse Museum Trust.

Tony Fouracre<br>October 1993

*Stone Creek*

# Pushing the Boat Out
(previously published in *The Helm*, 1969)

*I particularly want to include this article by my mother, Muriel Fouracre, which captures so tenderly, humorously and faithfully the annual launching of my first boat.*

It was on a misty October evening that the boat was pulled out of the Humber at Stone Creek, emerging like a whale from the deep, tilting perilously upward as Mr. Beal's tractor ground forward over the strip of beach optimistically known as the car park. The sun was sinking in a bed of rose colour, touching with beauty all the Immingham cranes and gas tanks, and hardly a breath stirred as the tide crept on over the shingle. *Pourquoi Pas* was then towed to the yard of the Pier Hotel, sheeted down for the winter, and passed into obscurity, as rugger and other activities claimed the attention of the crew.

But now it was April, and when she arrived at Stone Creek once more the mists and calms of the Autumn were long forgotten. A Force 6 (yachtsman's) gale was blowing from the SW, driving the usually mild Humber into real waves, tearing at the rank grass as the water seethed up to and over it, rattling the roofs of sheds and filling the sluices that regulate the flow out of the various Humber drains.

As a rule *Pourquoi Pas* slips gently off her trailer into the creek as the tide rises, but this time the wind would have blown her back again to the land, so once more the offer of Mr. Beal's tractor was accepted and she was literally pushed out into the mud, where one wheel of the trailer sank with speed, so that the owner and crew transferred themselves hastily to the other side of the boat to avoid capsizing.

All this time the gale banged and battered at crew and spectators, the smallest of whom, Paul, aged nearly five, lost his sou'wester for the third time. It was retrieved by a friend who tied a knot in the elastic, and was rewarded by a soft little voice asking if he could eat his tea in her car out of the wind. If he left his muddy boots outside, he could perhaps kneel up on the car seat and so watch all that was going on in *Pourquoi Pas?*

Whilst the crew waited for the tide to rise, operations in the boat were temporarily suspended, and, as Mr. Beal leaned against his tractor in case further help should be needed, the following conversation was borne on the wind:

Mr. B. shouting – 'Seen your pal lately?'

Owner, also shouting and wrestling madly with anchor chain – 'No – who?'

Mr. B. – 'Boat on that spit over there.'

Owner – 'Oh. Where's the wreckage?'

Mr. B. – 'Nowt left.'

Then, as the last speaker waved a farewell and went scrunching up the beach, *Pourquoi Pas* freed herself from her trailer. Tossing violently in the wind and waves, threatening every moment to be blown on shore again, she had to be hauled across the bow of the coble *Treasure*, riding head to wind at the mouth of the smaller creek where *Pourquoi Pas* had her mooring, and this manoeuvre could only be completed with much effect by hauling on *Treasure*'s mooring cable, and fending off by the crew, with imminent risk that *P.P.*'s dinghy would at any moment be crushed between the two boats.

By this time the youngest member had finished his tea, and wading into the encroaching tide looked so wistfully at the heaving boat that a kindly member of the crew spared a hand from his boat-hook to give the dinghy a deft shove Paul-wards. In a moment he had caught at the stern, scrambled in, and was hauled aboard by the rest of the crew, whilst the owner leaped into *Treasure*, slacking off her mooring rope so that *Pourquoi Pas* could be heaved under it, and so make the grade to her own mooring. By this time the exhausted and hungry crew had given up any idea of raising the mast that night, and finally came ashore after 8.00pm.

An uneventful journey homeward was only marked by Paul's falling asleep in his sou'wester, by the remark of an older spectator that he had missed the Archers, and a pause near Patrington to allow a hedgehog to proceed peacefully on his little stick legs under the nose of the car and across the road.

          Muriel Fouracre

# Humber Voyage
(previously published in *The Guardian*, 1963)

The recent westerly gales described by Professor Gordon Manley as accelerating down the eastern slopes of the Pennines do not appear to have lost their impetus when they reach the flat lands of East Yorkshire. They remind us of a similar series of depressions last August which must have upset a good many holiday plans. Our plan was to sail our auxiliary yacht, *Pourquoi Pas*, a Gibbs-built Sandmartin, from Stone Creek on the lower Humber up to York.

Knowing the limitations of the crew, my two sons Robert and Paul, and their friend, Edward, we delayed our departure for three days whilst winds of Force 6 upwards rattled the house. The fourth day, impatience and diminishing holiday time drove us to depart with the wind still SW F5-6.

One of the problems of sailing in the Humber is the very nasty chop which can arise in the reach above Hull, which under these conditions necessitates a beat to windward of 15 miles. Against the tide one can make no headway and, going upstream, it is a case of 'wind against tide', a phenomenon which has to be seen to be believed and is known locally as 'the holes in the water off Hull'.

The first couple of miles, during which we still had the shelter of the west bank, was decidedly uncomfortable, and from Thorngumbald Clough we made across river into wind to North Killingholme Haven which we have come to regard almost as a private harbour, having never encountered another boat there. It is a narrow channel just downstream from the oil jetty and dries out completely, but the 100-year-old New Inn is close at hand. Children on passage are soon bored and the crew were delighted at the prospect of exploring the shore, although walking them to East Halton brought many protests. Edward enlivened the afternoon by sitting atop a signpost whence he proclaimed to the world (two astonished cyclists), 'I am the King of Spain.' – a slight exaggeration, although his father does claim descent from an exiled Portuguese nobleman.

That evening the children made friends with the watchman at the shore end of the Fina Oil Jetty; even so, he would not allow them past his hut. 'Listen to the oil in the pipes,' he said. '2,000 gallons an hour going aboard that tanker.'

'Ever had a burst pipe?' asked the ever-curious crew.

'Yes, Christmas Eve, when the captain of a Norwegian tanker shut his valves whilst this end was still pumping. Mind you, he came ashore and apologised.'

The children went to their steeply tilted bunks on a boat cradled in black ooze and lay thinking of crude oil bursting out of a pipe at 2,000 gallons an hour, whilst the skipper renewed his friendship with Mick Thompson, the jovial proprietor of the New Inn.

Dawn brought another ragged, windy sky, but the wind seemed to ease a little as the tide came in. We left under triple-reefed mainsail and made up river in the lee of the Lincolnshire bank, scudding through the calm water and spilling much of the wind. A capsize here would most likely go unnoticed, and Humber sailing is very much self-help stuff so, discreet again, we turned into the next haven – East Halton Skitter. After only

Pourquois Pas, *my first yacht, off Stone Creek, May 1958.*

two miles of anxious exhilaration we were relieved to be in shelter, the more so as it was now so gusty that we had great difficulty in lowering sail. We subsequently learned that two cars had been blown right over while travelling on the nearest main road.

Two days and we still hadn't reached Hull! East Halton Skitter has a charm all its own. Not three miles from the centre of Hull, it is a completely isolated haven, a mile out of the main shipping channel. Nothing but cattle and birds for company ensure that it is visited only by wildfowlers and an occasional yachtsman from Brough Haven. 'Skitters' in Lincolnshire, 'Cloughs' in Holderness, and 'Pills' or 'Rhynes' in Somerset, all are land drains of which the tidal last few yards offer refuge for small boats from the roaring tides of the Severn and Humber.

As the boat dried out we clambered ashore, walking across the strays to Skitter Ness. Still the wind howled and the sight of the bigger ships battling towards Goole, their bows enveloped in spray, made us content to spend another night secure, though awkward on the mud. Next morning we made an attempt to catch the early tide but a shift of wind and a few feet too much of anchor chain put us squarely back on the mud for another ebb. This time, too far from the bank to go ashore, I had visions of mutinous crew – but in the unexpected way of boys they were completely absorbed by the test match commentary.

At half flood we were afloat, having decided to go downwind for comfort. We motored past Immingham with jib up and reached Grimsby at High Water: ten miles in two hours against the tide. 'Into the dock for a quiet level night,' I promised the crew.

Nosing up the slipway we were welcomed by the dock master, who apologised for the high dues for yachts. Determined on shelter and comfort at any price, we followed his directions: into the great sea lock only to stall our engine and to be ignominiously forced to walk through into Grimsby's enormous Royal Dock. We motored to the far end and berthed ahead of a large Swedish vessel, the *Aura,* whose bows towered some 15 feet above our masthead. Here the yacht lay in the shadow of the grotesquely neo-Gothic dock offices whose illuminated clock tower kept a benign moon face towards us through the night.

We walked back to the lock pit, about half a mile, and paid the friendly dock master our dues. His enquiry, 'Motor boat, is it?' brought a stout denial, but he remembered the auxiliary engine and cheerfully continued, 'We'll call it a motor yacht – it'll be a bit cheaper.'

He then asked us when we intended to depart. 'Don't be in a hurry to go,' he advised, remembering other North Sea battered yachts which had limped into his care. 'Firstly, it's rough outside, and, secondly, you've had to pay 20/4d and that's dearer – that's British Waterways – but after tomorrow you'll be on "dock rent" and that's only 1/8d a week.'

By now it was raining once more so we returned under cover of the vast unloading sheds, where dockers, rain shy, were playing indoor cricket. Our crew stood about helpfully fielding until they were offered a turn with the bat.

Five o'clock, and the dockers melted away, braving the rains to cycle into town. We followed and found in Riby Square a Gents complete with baths and a wash basin with free hot water and soap, quite a rarity in England.

Our night was calm but far from quiet. The trains with truckloads of Swedish wood pulp shunted till midnight and at 2.00am a tug, the *St. Cecilia,* plucked the *S.S. Aura* from the quay. I watched apprehensively from our cockpit, for a miscalculation of a few feet would have crushed *Pourquoi Pas* like a matchbox, but the tug handled the big vessel as gently as a basket of eggs. Two hours of peace were followed by more hooting and guttural German orders as the *M.V. Tilly Russ* from Hamburg moored in the vacant berth.

Next morning a shore excursion by bus to Cleethorpes, a fish and chip lunch, and, despite the prospect of extra days on dock rent, we left on the afternoon tide. The dock master showed us how to control the boat single-handed in the lock by means of one long rope made fast forward, led round a bollard and down to the helmsman. When the lock gates opened, the attendant neatly dropped the bight back on board.

The wind was still strong westerly so, discreet to the last, we set the jib and motored northbound across the estuary, soon reaching our sheltered channel behind Foulholme Sand with nothing more uncomfortable than a wildly swinging boom.

Four days, 20 miles, and our last port of call only five miles from base, still the final entry in the log epitomised the holiday: 'Crew damp, dirty, but in good heart.'

# Destination York

(previously published in *Humber Yawl Club Year Book,* 1964)

Our attempt to reach York by water three years ago was frustrated by strong westerlies which pushed us instead to Grimsby. This year, with twelve days at our disposal, the crew now older and more experienced and with a fresh boat, we tried again.

At Stone Creek with our Debutante, the *Annabel Louise,* we have the usual Humber tidal mooring problem of only being afloat a few hours either side of high water – and, even then we have to cross Holme Ridge to reach the shipping channel. High water saw us at Hull, and thereafter we slogged on with sails and outboard, taking two hours to do the last two miles against the ebb. To our delight the lock-keeper at Ferriby Sluice admitted us to the Ancholme four hours after high water.

We find that with a young crew – ours were Ed 16, Rob 13, and Paul 11 – a day's sailing, followed by a day's rest, works out well, so the second day they spent going sideways across the River Ancholme in the Gremlin we built last winter, as, by their mistakes, they gradually learned the art of dinghy sailing.

The third day we left in good time at one hour's flood. This was the earliest there was enough water outside the lock sill. The correct procedure according to the 'sailing directions' – nothing published anywhere, of course – is to set off with the flood and 'carry one's tide', up to Naburn in our case. The distances are vast by most yachtsmen's standards and, as the tide is later at each point up the river, it is in theory possible to keep up with the flood, although in practice we did not quite manage it.

Leaving the Lincolnshire side of Read's Island we crossed anxiously back to the shipping channel, for, although the Humber is a mile and a half across at this point 30 miles from the sea, the steamers keep meticulously to a channel 100 yards wide. The necessity for this was emphasised for us when we passed a barge, the *Humber Trader,* firmly aground not 300 yards from Upper Whitton float. The marks on her bow showed six feet of water!

The wind was perfect for us, NE F3, so we sailed happily on, keeping well to starboard at the Apex light to counteract the set of the current up the Trent. Past Blacktoft Jetty, where a coaster can wait for a tide for a berth in Goole docks, which we reached in three hours, and, having started our Seagull Century outboard, we stowed sail and lowered the 26-foot mast as the tide swept us under the railway bridge. The sailing was over for the time being and for our extensive motor trip we fitted a short home-made crutch in the tabernacle which enabled us to bring the mast foot forward to the bow and raise it clear of the deck hatch. As Rob steered us towards Boothferry Bridge I worked on deck with brace and bit securing this rig to the mast step. Looking up, I found to my horror that he had taken the wider, more obvious, but wrong, channel to the north of Hook Island. For an echo sounder we use a six-foot bamboo pole. This is marked in feet down to the draught of our boat (two feet three inches), and gives us enough warning of shoaling waters: seven feet or 70 are all the same to us. Our depth stick was down to the four-foot mark as we slid back into the tideway, and thereafter we navigated with more concentration, carefully keeping to the outside of the many bends.

We had the briefest glimpse of Selby and its abbey, as the tide carried us past the shipyard, past the barges clustered near the oil mills; we were too busy missing the piers of the rickety toll bridge. There was some satisfaction in not having to pay the toll but there is nowhere to moor with comfort in the tidal reaches of the Ouse or Trent, so it was imperative to reach the first lock in one tide. Once, we spent a night at anchor a little way up the Derwent, safe from the barge traffic, and another we lay bumping against Blacktoft Jetty, which is so high that our ropes wouldn't reach the gigantic bollards.

We reached Naburn lock eight hours after our start and comfortably before high water – 47 miles. 'The cheapest river in the country,' said the lock keeper as he charged us 3s for the *Annabel Louise* and 6d for the dinghy. Thereafter we had no tidal worries, and a mile upstream we secured to the bank at Acaster Malbis with enough daylight left to bathe before eating an enormous stew by the light of our Tilley lamp.

Then followed a week of idyllic motor boating. The thrill of tying up in the middle of York, where we suffered the embarrassment of having our motor stall just as we embarked friends on a river cruise. A blocked carburettor was quickly cleared – something we had learned earlier in the season when dirt in the petrol had caused us to miss a tide. Meanwhile our host unconcernedly pointed out the Guildhall with its ancient Watergate, although the crew seemed more interested in a youth intrepidly diving from the parapet of Ouse Bridge.

Our furthest point was Nun Monkton. We had hoped to reach Linton lock but were advised by a member of York Motor Boat Club that it was no longer working. Still, he very kindly loaned us a chart which gave the channel through the dreaded Linton Clay Huts. But long before we reached them we ran aground, and, having extricated ourselves by lightening ship and all hauling on a rope ashore, we promptly snapped our propeller spring on a submerged rock. Waiting for a spare delayed us for two days at Nun Monkton, but we could not have wished for a pleasanter spot. Here the Nidd joins the Ouse, forming a large deep pool, almost a natural marina. The River Nidd is fast flowing and shallow with a sandy bed ideal for bathing. We realised it was sandy when we saw a barge turn up the river. She was aground immediately, which was the skipper's intention, as he then proceeded to help himself to a cargo of sand from the river bed.

A few minutes walk through the wood was Nun Monkton itself, with its houses tidily arranged round a village green and the tallest maypole we have come across. The pub is called the Alice Hawthorn after a Shipton racehorse and here, over a pint, a local octogenarian reminisced of the days when he used to take a steam yacht with a five-foot six-inches draught as far as Ripon.

Our return journey to Naburn was another pleasant river cruise. A weekend was spent in York visiting the Minster, the Railway and Castle Museums and indulging in the luxury of a hot bath.

Returning down tide had problems which we could not postpone indefinitely. Although the Ouse ebbs for several hours longer than it floods, at low water spring tides one finds that some parts of the Humber channel are literally not deep enough for any vessel. When you leave at high water, the tide is ebbing away ahead and you cannot keep up with it as you can with the flood. This, of course, is because high water has occurred earlier along your route: for example, at Goole two hours earlier than high water at Naburn, and high water at Hull is one hour before Goole. Another difficulty for small craft is that there is no tidal berth or creek which one can reach at low water. A third problem for us was that the tides did not suit the hours of daylight too well.

We reasoned that, if we left Naburn at first light, we would have two hours of the ebb, anchor when we met the flood, and then continue. I put this to the lock-keeper who agreed it was possible but warned, 'It's a spring tide. There'll be a three-foot eagre.' Eagres on the Trent we knew, but it was news to us that the Ouse was so affected. The crew received this information with interest and mild apprehension. When it was likened to the Severn Bore, the youngest, confusing his terminology with that of shotguns, was convinced the proper name for this phenomenon should be the 'Three Bore'.

Next morning we arrived as the lock-keeper was extinguishing the gas lamps. Down, down he lowered us. The descent between slimy stone walls seemed endless, and when the lower gates opened we were in four feet of water, motoring down a chasm between muddy banks. The depth was fairly constant. We only touched bottom once, off the Wharfe's mouth.

The eagre arrived promptly at 9.30 when we were just below Cawood. Our drill had been rehearsed: kettle off, increase the motor speed and head straight into it. A three-foot wave is nothing at sea, but in the confines of a river it was most impressive. Breaking at its edges as it curled along the banks, there was a series of four waves advancing at seven or eight knots. Once the *Annabel Louise* had breasted them, we could make no progress over the ground so we manoeuvred into the bank and anchored. But the tide rose so fast that, within minutes, we were dragging. We paid out more chain and, using the rudder in reverse, steered into the bank once more so that we might breakfast out of the full force of the tide.

Never had the *Annabel Louise* travelled so fast through the water. Never was an anchor watch more needed. For two long hours our bowman fended off the driftwood, tree trunks and casks as they hurtled toward us on the tide. Well might he have been reminded of Jean Ingelow's lines:

> 'So far, so fast the eygre drave
> The heart had hardly time to beat.'

In two and a half hours the flood was spent and we were slowly on our way, slowed, we soon found, because we were dragging a mass of weeds and wreckage on our bilge keels. This cleared, we made good time to Selby. Here at the entrance to the canal British Waterways have thoughtfully provided a signpost. 'Goole 15 miles' gave us time for lunch and to prepare mast and sails for hoisting.

Off Goole the wind was W F4-5, so we were pleased to have raised the mast, set the sails and stowed the motor before we reached Swinefleet. 'Keep to the outside of the bends': at low water one can see exactly why.

The Humber was reached at 5.00pm with the ebb still running strongly. The Upper Whitton light vessel was sedately aground in four feet of water and a little further on a large tanker barge towered out of the water. 'Keep away. We're out of control,' the smartly boiler-suited petrol company's crew yelled dramatically. We altered course a little to oblige them, although they seemed rock firm on Whitton Sand. As we touched bottom ourselves, they cried, 'Look out. Here comes the eagre.'

The second eagre in one day makes one a veteran. Of course, in the wide reaches of the Humber it was no more than a six-inch ripple, enough though to allay our anxieties about the depth of water.

Enough too, to check our way, and, after half an hour, we abandoned our attempt to reach Read's Island, for, although we carried full sail when we should have reefed, the following wind was still not enough to carry us forward. We grounded briefly too. Touching bottom in the Humber is not to be recommended. With luck, on a rising tide one can steer bumping back into deeper water, provided one knows where deeper water lies. Once firmly aground, and in the swift running channels the bottom is iron hard, the situation changes with desperate suddenness. A high wind presses on sails which cannot yield, the swirling tide knocks the dinghy under the counter. For sure, the boat will heel alarmingly and perhaps fatally. One must have all sail off within seconds, but casting an anchor hopefully upon the waters is not without hazard as the chain may be swept under the boat and the set of the tide may be too strong to regain the anchor.

With these thoughts in mind we went about and returned with the flood tide to Brough Haven. Here at the Headquarters of the Humber Yawl Club we were greeted cordially and offered a berth at the Club's pontoon. Their elderly but active treasurer accepted our invitation and leapt nimbly aboard. Next morning he was at pains to give us a course to Wintringham Haven, which we visited briefly en route for Ferriby Sluice.

Our last day's sailing was our best. We covered the 20 miles from South Ferriby to Immingham in two and a half hours before prudence suggested we might be more comfortable under jib alone. We anchored off Grimsby and cooked a rolling lunch whilst waiting for the tide. At 5.30 we rehoisted the jib and reached across the estuary in a beam sea with a Force Seven wind. We were not anxious for the Debutante – only for the Gremlin astern – but a couple of water cans in her stern sheets kept the bow up and she managed by only charging us occasionally. In our narrow channel to Stone Creek we realised how strong the west wind was. Though aided by the spring tide, we could only make progress against it by full use of our engine.

It may be of interest to note our expenses for the trip. Other than food they were:

    Petrol 5 gallons    £1. 13s. 0d.
    Lock fees    18s. 4d.

Fresh milk was harder to obtain than fuel and our tactics varied from waylaying a milk roundswoman of South Ferriby to persuading a York riverside newsagent to order extra along with his own requirements. Ed, our self-appointed cook, was adept at combining tinned foods. We consumed £10 worth of these and, although the skipper began to weary of 'the baked beans with everything' routine, they are nourishing and filling – we soon found the large size is not as large as the family size. Tinned hamburgers were a great favourite but we did not live entirely out of tins: the cook tackled fresh steak and we ate our way through four dozen eggs.

Was it a success? At the end of the voyage the crew made a little speech of thanks to the skipper – something unheard of in our undemonstrative Yorkshire family.

# The Iron Bar

(previously published in *Humber Yawl Club Year Book*, 1966)

You wouldn't really think you could make a worthwhile story out of a piece of old iron, would you? Well, I mean anybody could put the facts down as they happened, but that wouldn't be interesting – much too rusty. But to clothe them with a metallic lustre, that's a challenge.

It all started with the undertaker at Easington – well, it really started at Blank's Boatyard, when they brought out a Mark II model with another 300 lbs of ballast on the keel; that made the Mark I owners think their Debutantes 'a bit skittish'. So I was looking for some scrap iron, but it always comes in such clumsy shapes: bedsteads, car sumps, old wheels. You can never find a nice squat solid piece of ballast, and I was talking about it to the undertaker; it wasn't because I thought he could supply a stiff, but because he's a joiner and was in the R.N.V.R. and is one of those boat chaps who's always building and tinkering and never puts to sea. In fact, in Harold's workshop, nearly hidden by coffin boards and pig troughs, is a magnificently made carvel planked, double-skinned mahogany speed boat – not quite finished. The engine's there too, under a pile of shavings. The boat has been there five years, but he never gets around to launching it. I sometimes wonder how he manages to finish the coffins in time for funerals, but, of course, there aren't very many of those.

Anyway, Harold knew where all the likely bits of iron were in 'East End'. Redvers Clubley, that inveterate collector of job lots, had some, but Harold was sure that either he would want an exorbitant price or more likely refuse to part with it at all, being driven by some inner compulsion to hoard kelter until it was impossible to find any particular items in his backyard. 'But Aly Newsom's the best bet – he has a lovely bit,' said Harold, talking very fast in what is almost a staccato stutter. 'Probably came off a ship, shouldn't wonder, it's in Sykes Bottom. Probably Aly's forgotten it's there.' We parted, Harold having agreed to ask Aly and to arrange for the iron to be brought to the roadside. I did not like to press him too hard, since he was doing me a favour, but I tactfully elicited its whereabouts and then walked from the Skeffling-Newton road down Sykes Lane and back to the Easington road, but without a glimpse of this six-foot length of iron.

Two weeks later I tackled him again. 'No good, never find it unless you knew just where to look,' he consoled. So seizing my chance, I asked him to come and fetch it with me then and there. 'Car's a bit small,' he said. 'I reckon it weighs a couple of hundredweight.' Undaunted, I drove him slowly over the brick rutted cart road to Sykes and there it was. I had walked over it unseeing, since it was being used as a main girder for a bridge across a dyke. We levered off the balk of timber covering it and then, Harold in the ditch and me on a rope, we moved first one end and then the other, and finally, by lifting one end between us, put it half in the car boot. The springs sagged alarmingly and Harold walked beside, as I drove the car at a snail's pace back to the road. It was a simple matter to drive it home, although dropping it out of the car made a thud which shook the house foundations.

George, our observant neighbour, came across, curious. So I prevailed on him to help me weigh it on the bathroom scales. Once round and a bit more: 'Twenty-three stone and you've broken my scales,' was the cry from the long-suffering lady of the house. 'And you've probably damaged the car too.'

It was clear that this heavyweight, measuring five feet long and four inches square, was unmanageable. 'Take it to Welwick blacksmith,' suggested George. 'He'll cut it in half.' We did, and he did – by dint of a little saw cut and a big smash with his heaviest hammer, revealing the crystalline cast-iron structure.

The next stage is the shameful one that affects all amateurs who fail to measure first. A glance round the inside of the boat made it embarrassingly clear that what was needed to fit exactly and snugly into the lowermost interstice were two pieces six inches shorter. So, humbly back to the blacksmith. Now that each piece weighed 11 stone, I was able to return alone and entreat the blacksmith to cut six inches off each. I sensed his displeasure at a difficult task which forethought would have rendered unnecessary. Smiting five feet of cast-iron is almost bound to crack it in two, but knocking six inches off is much less predictable. However, by dint of sawing and drilling first, he managed it.

Meanwhile, I had been busy making wooden chocks to stop any movement inside the boat and to transfer the weight directly to the keel. So now we are left with two pieces weighing eight stone and two 'light' pieces of three stone each – and even the light ones feel heavier each time I move them in the garage. The next stage is simple to describe, simply to lower them into the bottom of the boat, through the cabin companion way, without dropping them on board or overboard – but that is another chapter.

# Grimsby Race – Unfinished
(first published in *Humber Yawl Club Year Book*, 1967)

Those of us who keep our boats downriver from Brough have to make an extra effort to take part in the race. As we have to leave our moorings two tides before, we feel we have accomplished something even to have reached the start. The Alacrity and our Debutante, *Annabel Louise*, left Stone Creek on the early morning tide of Friday 7th July, waiting out the ebb in Humber Dock Basin and off Skitter Ness respectively. We met up for a walk ashore at South Ferriby before sailing on in company to Brough in time to enjoy the new shower facilities, a meal at the Ferry Inn and the evening bar session.

Despite pre-race talk of stopwatches and starboard tack starts, we found it the usual mad rush to stow our sleeping gear and, having

Debutante Annabel Louise, *my second boat, at South Ferriby, 1964. Self and two sons.*

14

motored out of the haven, had only time to unship the outboard and reef the mainsail before the starting gun. Still, we were not last over the line, which was an improvement on our previous entry.

On the run to the Lower Whitton we took out the reef and noted the Spurn Class yacht having some difficulty. The next run past Hull was all plain sailing, only marred by an inexpertly executed gybe round the Hebbles buoy which caused the crew of *Avian* a few moments anxiety. Thereafter things went less smoothly. On hoisting the spinnaker off Saltend the halyard parted. We lost the spinnaker boom overboard, although the spinnaker was retrieved undamaged. Unlike the canny skipper of *Monara* who put about to pick up his jib stick, we were so imbued with race fever that we carried on.

Deciding to take a short cut inside the channel off Killingholme, we found ourselves in company with *Avian* and *Samantha II* in very choppy water. At 11.30 approximately we dropped suddenly in the trough of a wave on to the iron-hard clay bottom of Foulholme Spit, striking it with our port bilge keel. There was an almighty crack and it was immediately obvious that water was coming in faster than we could remove it. The crew set to work with a bucket each and there was nothing for the skipper to do except encourage them and sail the slowly sinking boat to land. A quick survey decided us to make for the Cherry Cob Sands bank across the deeper channel by the Immingham deposit buoy, sailing as far downstream as our predicament allowed. We grounded thankfully at 11.45 off Stone Creek's Umbrella tree. The boat was well down by the head and in the cabin the water was lapping the starboard portlights. The outboard stowed in the stern locker had remained dry and we put this and some of the gear on the cabin top where we perched in the wind, eating sodden sandwiches whilst waiting for the tide to drop. We were on our own now although *Samantha II* had very kindly come across to inquire if we were alright.

As the tide receded, the damage became obvious – a three-foot crack in the plywood hull resulting from a twisting strain on the bilge keel. The twist had caused the plywood to spring apart and the two edges of the crack had overlapped.

Calculating that we had some two and a half hours before the tide returned we decided to walk ashore and obtain patching materials. We set off at a fair pace, carrying some of the gear, but as the mud became progressively softer we finished up on all fours, using our kitbags as hand supports. Twenty minutes hard graft to reach the bank where we left Elizabeth with the bedding. She had uncomplainingly baled out the cabin whilst all the floorboards and bunkboards had surged to and fro against her legs – and later she had the bruises to prove it.

Back at the boat, armed with fishboxes from the bank and a stone for a hammer, I plunged an arm into the flooded stern locker and managed to locate a pair of pliers with which we extricated the nails from the fish boxes. Arthur Allott, who had taken time off from his backyard building of his own Ballerina, split the cabin table top in two by main force and nailed it on the outside as I plugged the inside with surgical lint. The patching was completed in time to resume baling whilst awaiting the return of the tide. We knocked off for a breather when we came across the canned beer floating in the bilge. As the tide came in the south-west wind offset any tendency to drift upstream and we bumped slowly across the bank towards Stone Creek. Once at the highest point of the sand, we rigged the outboard and reached shore two hours before high water. We still had to bale as the leak was only reduced, and continued thus until the top of high water – six hours baling each.

We are really rather ashamed of our exploit, which was entirely due to faulty navigation by the skipper in what should have been familiar waters; we have only the satisfaction that we saved the boat by our own efforts. Perhaps some observation could be made for those who have never been in a foundering boat. Firstly, there is no room for any thought that suggests a yacht has buoyancy when badly holed. She goes down pretty fast, and offshore the only hope would be an inflatable dinghy. Secondly, patching materials are worth carrying aboard – for use inside and out: plywood strips, some sort of saw to shape them, iron nails to drive in quickly, a hammer and mastic. Fablon too has been suggested by one transatlantic sailor.

The tale has a happy ending, since the boat was fully repaired in a couple of weeks by Alan Worfolk at Sammy's Point, and we were relieved to find she is once again completely tight.

# First Time to Sea

(previously published in *Humber Yawl Club Year Book*, 1971)

We had been putting it off for 15 years. In that time, first in a Sandmartin and later in a Debutante, we had sailed the Humber from Spurn to Apex light and explored its tributaries – the Ancholme as far as Brandy Wharf, the Ouse to Nun Monkton and the Trent to West Stockwith. We had touched on every sandbank too.

This year two grown sons were persuaded to sign on as crew in our Hurley 22, *Mianti,* on the assumption that we should reach Holland, although it was the skipper's intention to be well satisfied with a cruise down the East Coast to Harwich.

We left Stone Creek at high water on Sunday 11 July after failing to finish in the Grimsby Race the day before. Heat haze and no wind. The ebb took us to Spurn and light airs from the south-east kept us tacking in visibility of 200 yards, despite which we managed to find Haile Sand, Rosse Spit and Protector buoys with nothing more exciting than encountering a balk of timber wedged under one bilge keel. After supper, cooked in still waters, we picked up the Inner Dowsing light bearing 120M.

At 23.00 the wind died altogether so we started our Johnson outboard motor and, on a direct course of 140M, during the night we identified N.E. Docking and North Race to starboard.

Before dawn a breeze came from the north, and in calm water with increasing wind we had an exhilarating sail until 04.30 when we reefed the main and changed to the storm jib. After a couple of hours the wind slackened enough for us to change back to No. 1 jib (until this season it had just been THE jib). At 08.00 with the wind NE F 3-4 the skipper went below to get his head down, as no one was feeling like breakfast, but the wind increased and the crew handed the jib again.

By the time Cromer was abeam it became apparent that the south-going flood and freshening NE wind were conspiring to set us on a lee shore. A decision was taken to make an offing and all that morning we thrashed out to sea, whilst the curve of the Norfolk coast unfolded ever eastwards. We estimated the wind to be F7 at the time but were told later that our sort of boat would not go to windward in F7. However, the wireless gave a gale warning and the seas were quite large so we roused the sleeping crew member and told him to put on his lifejacket which, much disgruntled, he did.

We concentrated on working to windward and came to bless our new storm jib, provided by Christopher Finch. At 14.30 we sighted NE Cross Sand buoy, confirming our offing of seven miles. We were then able to steer south down wind outside all the Yarmouth sandbanks, and at 16.30

we reached the South Scroby buoy (when the chart says in small letters 'seas break heavily' it really means it). By this time, despite the following wind, progress was slowed by the spring ebb, and we therefore turned into the Hewitt channel to pass inshore of Holme Sand to Lowestoft where we tied up at 17.00.

The well-known hospitality of the Royal Norfolk and Suffolk Yacht Club restored our weary bodies, although the club premises were full of harassed owners of 14-foot boats which had come to grief in the day's racing of International Fourteen Week. Amid all this coming and going of colourful continental and transatlantic dinghy sailors, the Club secretary sat imperturbably at his desk checking positions and damages: perhaps it was Force Seven after all.

All that afternoon we had in sight Winterton tower and Yarmouth South Denes power station, two excellent land marks.

Distance run: Stone Creek to Lowestoft 107 miles in 33 hours.

We spent the following day at the Lowestoft seaside watching the dinghy racing, and 06.00 on Wednesday 14 July saw us making up against the half ebb, bound for Harwich in a light westerly breeze. The channel is close inshore to the south of Lowestoft and we were able to escape some of the tide. Off Pakefield we made out to sea to clear the Barnard shoal before setting course 200M to the most conspicuous Sizewell power station. At mid-day the wind was South F3-4 and we were standing on and off shore with the flood tide helping us along the coast. By this time the crew were feeling quite seasoned and even undertook the repair of the port winch whose ratchet was slipping. We put out to sea again to clear Aldeburgh Ridge and Orford Ness and sighted Shipwash light vessel at 14.30. Soon the large container cranes at Felixstowe identified Harwich, where we contrived to arrive just after high water and had a busy hour beating into the harbour just as every packet was either arriving or sailing. 'Not like the Humber, no tides here,' I encouraged the crew – but it was a long two hours beat up the Orwell to Clamp House where we secured to a buoy for a supper break. On the north shore there is a new marina developing, but it seemed rather far from anywhere else by road. Later we motored up to Pin Mill but the tide was too low for us to go ashore until next mooring, by which time the coastguard had posted us overdue since we had been observed coming into Harwich and then lost. Our phone call cleared their CG66.

Distance made good: Lowestoft to Harwich 42 miles in 12 hours.

The next three days were spent sailing up the Orwell to Ipswich, down to Harwich and up the Stour with NW winds F4-6. From Mr. Ward, the chandler at Pin Mill, we obtained free water, hired a dinghy for 25p per day and a mooring for 25p a night. The former enabled us to visit the Butt and Oyster each evening and the latter to sleep soundly at night.

Sunday 18 July we left Pin Mill at mid-day half ebb after going to church at Chelmondeston to hear the Bishop of Dunwich (we did not know there was one). All the local boats were out and, as we approached the Deben, we were overtaken by several Pandoras, which seemed to be their racing class. The Deben bar is notably tricky. 'Never go in on the ebb,' is the local advice. Leading marks are moved as necessary. The boats seemed all to be taking a course to the north of the bar and we followed suit, sluicing in with a fair wind and tide. In fact, on our way out next morning, we found they had all taken a subsidiary channel. Once inside, we were so pleased to be overhauling a Trident that we missed the buoy marking Horse sand which was fortunately well covered.

After anchoring off Ramsholt Quay for the night, we paddled perilously ashore in our Campari as did the crew of a neighbouring Vivacity of W & F.S.C. which stands for Walton and Frinton Sailing Club, where, like us Stone Creekers, they moor in mud to their own old gas stoves and tractor wheels. Ramsholt church is 14th-century, has an oval flint tower, and the pub has that terrible East Anglian ale. On the Deben we noticed a Debutante, for which we always we have a soft spot, and also Gipsy Moth III.

Next day, after putting our archaeologically minded crew member ashore to hitch hike to Sutton Hoo, we motored out of the Deben through the proper channel and sailed easily to Lowestoft with a following wind. Thirty-nine miles in seven hours, for five of which we had our little spinnaker pulling.

Tuesday 20 July we left Lowestoft 06.30 and, with no wind, we motored against the tide. At 08.30 the crew were surveying the talent already displayed on the Yarmouth beaches. A long slog, mostly motoring, up the Norfolk coast took us until 21.30 when we anchored off Wells, not liking to essay the entrance at dusk on a falling tide.

Days run: 53 miles in 15 hours.

After an hour's snooze the skipper awoke to hear the breakers nearer and, as the leading lights seemed a lot closer, we motored a mile to the NE before anchoring in six fathoms with all our chain plus a good scope of rope. We were up at 04.30 and found a coaster anchored half a mile away. We were glad we had a riding light until we later found he had not noticed it. Wells approach is not obvious: the pilot talks of leading lights but does not stress that these are quite close inshore and that, after picking up the black conical bar buoy, you should next leave two black beacons to starboard, then make for the leading lights in line, leaving two more black buoys to starboard.

We met the harbour master leaving to pilot in the coaster and he directed us to tie up alongside a ship at the quay. This was quite a comfortable berth, enabling us to climb ashore across the coaster – one foot of water at low water – until the evening, when it was decided to turn the coaster, his stern rope snapped and the three-knot flood took charge, so we had to motor smartly into mid-stream to avoid being crushed against the quay.

Thursday 22 July we left Wells 07.30 just before high water and on clearing the bar set course 345M motoring in poor visibility. After two hours there was enough wind to switch off the motor and we altered course to 315M to allow for the eastward tide set. We sighted SE and NE Docking buoys at appropriate intervals and at 13.15 the Inner Dowsing came up dead ahead. A course of 345M took us between D.Z. 7 and the Protector to Rosse Spit. We made our landfall at Spurn at 20.45 in deteriorating visibility but fortunately an increase of wind to F3 NNE and full engine enabled us to make up against the ebb to lie for the night inside Spurn before making the final leg to Stone Creek on the morning tide.

Distance run: Wells to Spurn 53 miles in 14 hours.

Although the total of 360 miles was accomplished at an average speed of only 3.5 knots, we are well pleased with the Hurley's performance and, of course, we are secretly congratulating ourselves on having managed 12 consecutive days without running aground anywhere.

*Mianti, a Hurley 22', my third boat, with a new mainsail, 25 May 1975: self and Laurie Kell.*

# An Anglo – Dutch Friendship
## (1991)

The first seeds were sown (literally) in 1953. In January that year floods devastated the coast of Holland with much loss of life and also affected the English coast as far north as Sunk Island. There the land was either inundated or the sea water backed up the drains, making the land too salty to use. The official policy of the Ministry of Agriculture was advice to farmers to leave the land fallow for two years until the salt leached out and to offer a small compensation.

Harry Dixon, an ebullient farmer, would have none of this and telephoned the more knowledgeable Dutch Government. He was put in touch with a farmer from the island of Tholen: Ir Geuze. Mijnheer means Mister but Ir is the highly respected title of Engineer. Ir Marine Geuze, besides being on various government committees, has also founded a farmers' co-operative sugar beet factory.

With the Dutch advice, which included the copious use of gypsum, Harry was able to produce a crop the first year. Marine Geuze was later pleasantly surprised to receive an invitation to visit Harry at Old Hall Farm and to bring all his family. Holidays abroad were unusual in those post-war days and he accepted. When he asked why, Harry replied in his blunt Yorkshire way, 'Because you have saved me £1,000, that's why,' – again quite a lot of money in those days.

Harry had no young children, so arranged for the Geuze children – Annie, Reint and Marinus, to meet with his relations, the Nordons, the Todds and the Fouracres. Marine's wife Ellie, with charming Dutch directness, said, 'What are your children's ages? Let us make the exchanges.' Thus it came about that Annie stayed with the Todds at Shrubbery Farm, Reint with the Nordons, and Marinus junior with the Fouracres. Later Gillian and Susan Todd, Tina Nordon and Paul Fouracre visited Zandhoeve in Tholen, and later still Marinus worked on Old Hall Farm during his holidays, commenting that he was overworked and underpaid! The grown-ups also visited each other's houses.

We had often talked of visiting Tholen by boat. Our first attempt was in 1974 in our seven-metre Hurley. Paul and I sailed from Stone Creek to Lowestoft to be joined by Dave Suddaby of S.S.S. Marine. We made a landfall at Vliessingen and motored up the Kanaal door Walcheren to Middelburg. Marinus drove to see us, took us to Veere, and next day we visited Tholen, taking the train to Roosendaal.

Our next trip was in 1987. I now had an eight-metre yacht *Cracker*. I had just retired and with my partner, Duncan Busfield, and his wife, Bettine, we took part in the Hull-Breskens North Sea race. We then cruised the Oosterschelde, staying two nights in the marina at Sint

Annaland in Tholen. Here we were entertained by young Marinus, who now runs the farm at Poortvliet. Marine senior lost his first wife but has now retired and re-married, living at Wouw. He and Evalina have 18 grandchildren between them. On that occasion we met Reint, now from Groningen, and his son, Tijmen, who collects stamps, so he and I have corresponded.

In 1990 *Cracker* again raced to Breskens, again coming last. This time with Tony and Karen Johnson we finally reached the harbour of Tholen itself via Middelburg, the Veersemeer, the Oosterschelde and the new Bergsche Diepsluis. Marinus took us by car to Wouw. At Markt 10, Marine and Evaline live in what was formerly the doctor's house. Marine has the doctor's consulting room as his study.

This summer with Doctors Wallace and Pamela Portal as crew I again reached Sint Annaland and met up with the Geuze family for supper at the farmhouse and an evening walk along the dijk. This is very reminiscent of Sunk Island. The farm no longer has livestock. Marinus grows potatoes which he stores at a controlled temperature and humidity until he judges the market to be right. This year he was also growing cauliflowers for seed and tulips and peonies for bulbs. He had hoped to sail back with us but, because of the cold spring, his early potatoes were late and he could not leave them. So next day we took him and his friend Marianne for a sail from Sint Annaland to Bruinisse.

Earlier this year Jane and I stayed in Wouw on our way back from Spain. Marine was pleased to show us the Sint Annaland museum of which he is chairman. A former industry in Tholen was the growing of madder – *Rubia tinctoria* – the root was crushed to produce the red dye. There were several mills for this and the museum features it.

Whenever the Geuzes are in England they keep up contact with the Todds, Harry Dixon's son, George, the Nordons and the Fouracres.

Long may the friendship continue.

# Across the North Sea
(written 1982)

Offshore voyages from the east coast of England usually make for Scandinavia or the Netherlands. Because the North Sea funnels to the south, the longer, more exposed, crossings are in the north. Arctic winds enhance the funnel effect so that the southern part can experience a build-up of waves which the shoal waters aggravate.

Our winter plans and spring preparations were to make an initial 170-mile open passage in waters nowhere deeper than 90 feet. The crew was to be son Paul and his wife Jo.

Our boat, *Cracker,* a 26-foot Westerly Centaur, lies at Stone Creek. Fifteen boats are mud-berthed at this tiny natural harbour on the River Humber which has a tidal rise and fall of 15 feet. Imagine our consternation on the morning of departure when we found the tiller lines had come adrift and the rudder was jammed. A quick dip over the side confirmed the upper edge of the rudder was catching on the underside of the hull. The shaft had bent backwards – possibly because there is no lower pintle – as the boat slipped forward whilst taking the mud.

By now the radio waves on our newly installed V.H.F. set were crackling with good advice so a decision was made to beach *Cracker* at Spurn Point, a finger of sand at the mouth of the Humber which has a sheltered up-river side. Here we were offered help by the life-boat crew. The repair proved simple. We filed off a quarter of an inch from the top of the fibreglass rudder and were able to straighten the shaft with a rope under the hull between the bilge keels, up through the bow fair lead and back to a winch.

Our departure from the mouth of the Humber took place, therefore, when we refloated on the evening tide of Saturday 10 July, motor-sailing on a course 115 magnetic into a head wind F2. At dusk we lowered sail, and our Volvo Penta diesel ran uncomplainingly through the night on a gallon of fuel every two and a half hours.

At night we have two-hour watches, the crew standing the early and late turns, the skipper the middle two hours of darkness. July in these latitudes is fully dark from 23.00 to 03.30.

The powerful beam of the Dudgeon Light Vessel was visible for most of the night and we had the light vessel abeam by dawn – 45 miles in ten hours. Our next marks of interest were the towering platforms of the Leman natural gas field, which we reached mid-morning. As the south-going tide took us close to one platform, the safety boat *Dreadnought* sent off an inflatable with a message:

'Your position is 54°0.6' north 02° 11.0' east. Forecast, wind easterly, fog. Bon Voyage.'

And the crewman added, 'Please stay 500 metres clear of the rigs.' – quite the friendliest of admonitions. I thanked the skipper on the V.H.F. He assured us that every platform had its own safety boat and would be glad to check on our progress.

The second night was less comfortable, although we were sailing well, but the anxiety of the initial setback with the rudder and two disturbed nights clouded the skipper's judgement so that he did not believe a radio bearing on Schiphol aero-beacon. Thus our landfall was at Zandvoort some seven miles south of our destination, Ijmuiden, which has tall chimneys which we could not see in the poor visibility. However, a friendly Dutch yacht directed us to the north.

Forty-three hours to Ijmuiden. We had been warned about the strong tide across pier heads but, once inside, we motored the mile to the locks in increasing shelter. Yachts can find temporary mooring outside the locks to the south in the fishing harbour. The smallest of four locks, the Kleinensluis, is recommended for small boats, but as the Middensluis was open we slipped in alongside a Dutch yacht returning from Yarmouth, a large coaster, and an enormous Rhine sand barge. Once through the lock, we waited in the hot sunshine to clear Customs who showed far less interest than that aroused by a crossing from the U.S. into Canada.

The Nordzee Kanaal is remarkable. Thirteen miles to Amsterdam. Depth 49 feet, width 510 feet. We motored along, having a large stew for a late lunch – our first solid food for 24 hours – in company with a huge bulk carrier in the charge of four tugs. People fished and picnicked on the banks, yachts and dinghies sailed back and forth, youngsters in rubber boats splashed perilously, escorted by ducks and swans. Despite what appeared to be its vast size, the Dutch say the Kanaal is not deep enough for the large modern ships and shake their heads over the decline of Amsterdam as a port overtaken by Rotterdam. At each kilometre there is a marker post. Hemberg Bridge is at K7 and here we had to wait an hour since priority was given to the commuter rail traffic. The kanaal leads through the centre of Amsterdam where it is busy with barge traffic and ferries crossing. In the Sixhaven marina, which is just opposite the central station, we found a berth with electricity and water for a mere three dollars a night.

The crew were impressed to find our Dutch contact, Hank, and his wife on the jetty to meet us. He proved a delightful host, taking us first to the Central Post Office to phone home and then for drinks, sitting in the Leidsplein, watching the busy city life. Dutch phone boxes are simplicity itself.

Next day we pursued our various interests and met up for a meal in the evening with Hank and Elena, followed by a tour of canals by waterbus. At dusk each bridge is magically framed in lights. The Dutch seem paranoiac about pickpockets and vandals, which we concluded was because they were relatively new experiences for them. I caught the anxiety and carried my wallet clutched inside the engine tools' ditty bag.

Two days in Amsterdam was scarcely enough. On the second, our neighbouring berth was occupied by fellow Humber Yawl Club members in the 30-foot Starlight. They had crossed to the Frisian Islands and come south through Ijssellmeer.

On 14 July we departed at 09.00, continuing west through the heart of Amsterdam dockland to the Oranje Sluis, which leads to the Ijssellmeer. This is an enclosed arm of the sea. The fresh water gives perfect inland sailing over an area of 50 miles by 15, with depths averaging six feet. The extent has been reduced by land reclamation which the Dutch do by enclosing parts with dijks, thus creating polders. There are plans for further polderisation but vociferous conservationists, agonising over the effect on the ecology, have caused a stalemate. A brief reach across the southern end took us to Muiden, which is approached along a narrow channel and is the headquarters of the Royal Netherlands Yacht Club. Here we saw a fleet of traditional Dutch Botters and tied alongside one whilst we went ashore for provisions. Dutch towns and villages all seem to be picturesque, the buildings typified by stepped gables.

We anchored offshore in the lee of Pampus Island for a picnic after bathing overside. Pampus Island was originally one of the notorious sandbanks which medieval sailors had to avoid when the only approach to Amsterdam was from the north via the Zuider Zee, as it was formerly called. We were enjoying high pressures with constant north-easterlies which gave us a fast ten-mile sail to Volendam. The low-lying shores are inconspicuous but Marken Lighthouse is an excellent land mark. Volendam is another former fishing port – now tideless – but it still has a thriving fish quay. Moorings are crowded and there were four boats between us and the quay. For this we were charged £1.

Overnight a warm front passed, bringing rain and a 180° wind shift. Next morning, after buying smoked mackerel and a Volendam fisherman's cap, we hoisted our spinnaker. Volendam, Marken, Urk and Edam, now on the shores of the Ijssellmeer, were all originally islands which have developed and preserved different costumes. Our daily routine was a passage of 10 to 15 miles during which we anchored for a swim and lunch. On this occasion we practised man-overboard drill and swimming in life-jackets – impossible except on your back.

Hoorn is yet another medieval town. The museum is a splendid example of 16th-century Dutch architecture. Local children were diving off the lock gates, which are no longer used. Here I was able to have the broken brackets of our boarding ladder repaired: both phosphor bronze hooks had snapped. When I asked the engineer if it would be easier to replace them in steel he replied in good English: 'Not easier but much stronger.'

From Hoorn to Enkhuizen was another 11 miles with a following wind. The Ijsselmeer is divided by a dijk or bank which carries a road 16 miles to Lelystad. There are locks at either end and the approach to Enkhuizen is marked by brightly flashing leading lights. We negotiated the lock quite easily as we now considered ourselves experienced, having learnt that a yacht should allow the bigger commercial traffic to enter and leave first, so avoiding the turbulence from their very powerful screws.

Enkhuizen also has an old harbour and a new marina with more facilities at a higher cost, although everywhere we were impressed by the encouraging attitude towards boating and the modest charges. In the Buitenhaven (outer harbour) we were directed to a berth by the Harbour Master from the inflatable in which he sat at a centre steering console which contained his V.H.F. and his cash desk. The town is larger, with good shops and restaurants, stalls were selling *nieu haring* (pickled herring) and *paaling* (smoked eels). There were ship repairing facilities, and the Zuider Zee museum in the Peper Haus, an old warehouse. The museum is devoted to the ancient traditions of the fisherfolk and their craft. There is a Hall of Boats, excellent models of the different fishing methods, and rooms furnished in the styles of the different townships. I was pleased to confirm that my Volendam cap was a faithful reproduction, even though it had been made in China. After supper I walked along to the harbour entrance on a warm still night. Though dusk, yachts were still crowding in. There were many of the traditional Botters with their vast lee boards. These seemed to be charter boats with young crews, all very friendly.

Next day we crossed to Staveren for one night before coming back to Den Oever where there is the lock at the south-eastern end of the Afsluit Dijk out into the Wadden Zee. Now we could put away the Water Karten 1810 of the Ijssellmeer in favour of 1811 of the Wadden Zee. These invaluable charts have large-scale insets of each harbour and clearly mark the channels. We timed our arrival at Den Oever to catch the last of the ebb down the Wierbalg channel. This is narrow, with least depth of six feet, but is well buoyed. Of our crew, Paul is an experienced seaman and good helmsman but colour-blind, whereas his wife, Jo, has perfect sight, mastered in meteorology, and never missed a buoy or weather forecast.

From Den Oever to Oudschild on the island of Texel is 12 miles. We anchored in a flat calm on the edge of the Bollan sand in four feet so I was able to bathe and photograph the boat. Texel is flat – 16 miles by four, so a hired bicycle is the obvious way to explore it. The western beaches of the Friesian Islands confront the North Sea, and the eastern side give on to a maze of tidal channels between sand banks, well described in *Riddle of the Sands*.

At Oude Schild there is a fishing fleet of trawlers and a new Jacht haven where the club house is an old steamship. We had an evening meal at the house of Jo's friend, Daniel, a Czech who works at the Oceangraphic Institute. We arranged to take his family for a sail next day but strong winds changed our plans. Instead, we entertained them to lunch on the boat, and, as they walked to the harbour entrance to wave us farewell, we put on a show, leaving under full sail for Den Helder. This is the premier Dutch naval port with very good facilities for yachts. We locked through into the Binnenhaven, which is also the beginning of the Nord Holland Canal. We stayed at a yacht club run by the non-commissioned officers of the Dutch Navy. More friends took us out for an evening meal, having arranged for an Indonesian *Rijs Tafel* at Bergen-Am-Zee. Jan, who had been in the navy, explained that, when the Dutch colonists found that the Indonesians lived on a monotonous diet of rice, they taught them to embellish it with many spicy side dishes.

Even now in every ship in the Dutch Navy the invariable menu is:
Monday. Pea soup followed by *Naze Goering*.
Wednesday. *Rijs Tafel*.

We had intended to spend an extra day in Holland, but the early morning shipping forecast was of a persisting high with north-east F4-5 – the prevailing winds are Atlantic Westerlies. 'The wind is fair for England. We go today,' I told our Dutch neighbour, who cautioned, 'Scheveningen radio says Force 6-7.' We left at noon, took the ebb through the Molengat Channel, leaving the Norder haaks zand dry to port – two rolls in the main and No 2 jib, course 285° magnetic.

A beam wind all the way gave us a fast sail, and after 24 hours a distant glimpse of the Norfolk coast suggested we had not allowed enough for leeway. Now we were in familiar waters off the treacherous Wash. Our course was via Dudgeon and the Inner Dowsing light tower. The whole passage from Den Helder to the Humber took 35 hours, starboard reach all the way except when I asked the disbelieving crew to change tack in order to return to the No. 2 jib for the night. Putting-about is an easy way to heave-to and a jib, which is thus aback, can be lowered by the foredeck man in relative comfort. We needed a further three hours to motor sail the last eight miles to Grimsby against the ebb. Here we anchored for a couple of hours before crossing the estuary to our beloved Stone Creek in a drizzle which heralded the end of the fine spell.

In a memorable 12 days we had covered 453 miles, run our diesel for 43 hours and used 12 gallons of fuel.

# Cruising the East and West Schelde
(previously published in *The Helm*, 1987)

*Cracker*, our 26-foot Centaur, reached Breskens by way of the 1987 R.M.A. race but the less said about our performance the better, although, despite motoring from Cromer, we were allotted a courtesy tenth place.

Breskens is an ideal port of entry for Holland. It is accessible at all states of tide. The full facilities include an extensive chandler's where we replaced our winch handle, and there was no overnight charge for visiting racing crews. On Tuesday 7 July, after a lunch of rollmops, smoked eels and new bread in bright sunshine, we motorsailed the three miles to Vlissingen, crabbing to buck the fast ebb. Shipping abounds on the Westerschelde and the large ferries cross in both directions half hourly. After circling in the harbour entrance we entered the lock on two greens – having it to ourselves. We were not charged at any of the locks. The Kanaal Door Walcheren leads out of the inner harbour and there are four bridges to negotiate before Middelburg. Here we found the harbour master's office just before the bridge to the inner harbour, whose opening times are prominently displayed.

Once tied up to the quay wall, we walked into the restored medieval city admiring especially the Stadhuis. After an Indo-Chinese *Rijs Tafel* – a real blow-out recommended by the skipper who had been before – we turned in to be suddenly awakened when a drunken Dutch youth jumped the six feet down from the quay to land heavily on our foredeck. Duncan was up in a flash to repel boarders, only to find himself looking up at another ten burly Dutchmen from two chartered yachts. All became clear when the arm of the twelfth rose eerily out of the dark water under our bow!

Wednesday July 8, after a morning in town sampling *Appelgebak met Slagroom* and climbing The Lange Jan tower to view the countryside, we refuelled at a convenient tanker barge and motored into wind to Veere – one is not allowed to tack on the canals. Immediately after locking into the Veersemeer we moored at a yacht station on the last bit of the canal and walked into Veere. All the old Dutch towns we visited were once open to the sea and all are marked on the 17th-century map. They are fortified, often with a moat which was originally an arm of the sea. There was another good chandler's with Inland Waterways charts. Surprisingly on show was a Pebble Sailer made at Brandesburton. The huge church, which is a good landmark, was used by Napoleon to stable his horses. The Veersemeer, which is stagnant salt water, is ideal inland sailing. It measures 14 miles long by one mile wide and the banks and islands are mostly nature reserves with many jetties and remote harbours for which there is no charge – very peaceful.

The Dutch Delta project's first major undertaking was to exclude the sea from the Veersemeer in 1961 with the Veerse Gatdam. The intention then was to enclose the East Schelde with a five-mile dijk from Walcheren to Schouwen but it took 20 years to resolve the opposing views of the ecologists, the sea defenders and the drainage authorities. A large enclosed lake like the Ijsellmeer would become stagnant salt water. This would destroy the shellfish industry, which is a vast local interest. Finally, in 1987, the Pijlerdam-Oosterschelde was completed. These are two-mile-lengths tidal barriers which can be lowered to contain storm surges with two artificial islands, one of which has a lock to the North Sea – the Roompot Sluis. The effect of this has been to reduce the tidal range by one-third.

After a night at a jetty, a swim and a walk ashore, we sailed three miles to an island where we moored for lunch before a leisurely sail under genoa to Zandcreek. Here we locked into the Oosterschelde after waiting for an enormous Ford barge with three decks of cars and tractors. The Ossterschelde is understandably a favourite cruising ground: clear water, reasonable tides and many harbours. With the wind NW F3-4 we tacked toward the Zeeland Bridge which, with 53 arches, is the longest in Holland. There is a lifting section at the northern end which opens on the half hour. We waited for the 18.00 opening and, after motoring the mile-long sea canal, spent the night in Zierikzee, another fascinating ancient moated port in Schouwen.

Friday 10 July we continued our habit of a morning in the town and an afternoon sail to the next port. We visited the town hall and the maritime museum which was formerly the prison. Here we saw the wooden walls adorned by the prisoners' carvings of women's shoes, which were their sex symbols. We discovered that *oosterpannen* was a method of putting roof tiles in the water, to which the oysters attached themselves. I also explored a working wind cornmill.

We left to catch the 13.00 bridge opening but, as it was half flood, we sailed under a fixed span with about one-metre clearance. It seemed less, and Bettine stayed in the cabin 'to be safe'. The NW wind took us quickly up the Keetaan into Krabbencreek to Sint Annalan on the island of Tholen for a late lunch. This is a good marina and inexpensive. We spent two nights here visiting with friends who have a farm on the island. They drove us to Bergen-op-Zoom, took us swimming and gave us a barbecue.

Sunday July 12 we took the last two hours of the spring ebb and at low water beached *Cracker* for an hour off the west shore of Tholen, bathing and cleaning the topsides. When the tide turned we had a pleasant spinnaker run up the Brabansche Vaarwater into Oosterschelde proper to Yserke. There must have been 1,000 yachts apleasuring and we saw at least ten Centaurs.

The Oosterschelde now finishes at the east end of Tholensch Gat. The little port of Tholen is now landlocked so they have made a new Bergsche Diepsluis which gives access to the Rijn Schelde Kanaal and also to Bergen-op-Zoom. Yserke has two yacht harbours and one fishing harbour, with some 200 fishing boats. It is the centre of the oyster and mussel industry and the banks are lined with fish-keeping tanks and processing plants. At DFL15 a night it was the most expensive mooring – about the same as South Ferriby.

We departed next morning at 06.45 to catch the first of the ebb to Wemeldinge where there are three locks into the Kanaal Door Zuid Beveland. This is very commercial but a useful cut across to the West Schelde. We were one hour in transit, taking breakfast as we travelled to Hanswert. This is very busy and we shared the lock with six barges. We were assigned a place by loud hailer. Allowing the barges to go first, we were in some doubt as to how an enormous barge directly astern could nose out. It had not occurred to us that he would have a bow thruster. They are building a second lock here.

The West Schelde was ebbing strongly and we were at Terneuzen by 10.45. This is the third largest Dutch port and there are locks into the ship canal to Ghent. One has to watch out for the fast tide across the entrance of the harbour upstream of the locks. Here there are two marinas. We chose the more westerly and found it quiet, adequate and cheap at DFL8.50 with free hot showers. In the afternoon the temperature of the air was 29°C and the water 21°C.

Next morning the 11 miles to Breskens were accomplished in two hours via the southern subsidiary Hoofd Plaat Channel which avoided the large vessels. An afternoon swim from the beach was followed by a final celebration in the Breskens clubhouse restaurant. A dish of mussels with Breton sauce was more than I could manage. I later discovered that one portion was 2.0 kg of mussels.

Our lasting impressions are an excellent cruising ground, friendly people and well buoyed channels.

Crew: Duncan and Bettine Busfield.

# Nipper, the Luff!

(previously published in *The Helm*, 1990)

In my 20 years as Auxiliary Coastguard and member of the Rocket Crew we never had the satisfaction of a real Breeches Buoy rescue from a ship ashore. But we practised our drill with rocket and hawser assiduously.

The commands were precise as befits a naval based drill. When the hawser along which the Breeches Buoy travels was secured to the wreck – in practices to a post in a field at Holmpton – the 16-man crew hauled it taut and then set up a tripod. The hawser was a three-inch right-hand-laid Manilla rope with a five-ton breaking strain. To achieve the final tension needed to raise the sagging line out of the water, a purchase was rigged. The order, 'Haul taut!' was followed by: 'Avast hauling. Nipper the luff!'

Then it was the task of No. 11, Leader of the hawser section, to secure a bight of tackle around the three iron stakes previously hammered into the ground by the anchor section. He then reported, 'Luff secured,' and tended it throughout the wreck service.

It was not until a recent visit to the Greenwich Maritime Museum that I discovered the origin of the order whilst watching a video on cables and anchoring. In the old men-of-war the anchor was raised by manpower on the capstan. In Nelson's *Victory* the capstan was double, going through two decks. The massive 23-inch circumference anchor hawser was too thick to go round the capstan, and therefore a smaller capstan rope was used. The luff of this was taken forward and made fast to the main hawser just inboard of the hawse hole – a very confined area. As the hawser came aboard this manoeuvre had to be repeated, so a very small nimble youngster had to hurry forward and re-secure the capstan rope luff, the order being: 'Nipper, the luff!'

This is the origin of children being referred to as: Little Nippers.

### Postscript – by others

*One of Tony's secrets has been revealed!*

*He has the Queen's Long Service medal for 'standing by' for 20 years in the Coastguards.* [Anita Rowland]

*(Such an award, as you all know, was always referred to in the services as '20 years undetected crime'!)* [Brian Nordon]

# Last and First

(previously published in *The Helm*, 1991)

A winter lay-up lends poignance to the last sail of the season. Sometimes it is a non-event as October gales give way to November fogs and you realise your last decent sail was in August.

Last year I was lucky. Returning from a September holiday in Spain I encountered one of the anticyclones which have been a feature of our most recent autumn and spring. High pressure at this time of year can mean lack of wind and fog but on 17 October the barometer stood at 1028 and the wind was SW, a cool day with no cloud.

*Cracker* was through the lock two and a half hours after high water and was soon spanking along past Saltend with the full ebb and a wind forecast at SW F5-6 decreasing 4. A reefed main and No. two jib was a comfortable combination. The genoa had been under repair and the No. one jib I had sold to Trevor Dalby.

Single handing on the Humber with a roller reefing jib and an autohelm need be no hassle for the elderly. Once during a bout of over-confidence I even rigged the spinnaker, but fortunately ran out of water off Reads Island before I had time to hoist it. (It is not so much the hoisting but the lowering which frightens me.)

Spurn was reached in two and a half hours. The anchorage is seldom straightforward under sail. I lowered the main as I passed the lifeboat and was just able to make up over the south-going tide so that I could let fly the jib and drop the anchor in one fathom.

Three-quarters of an hour for the usual uncomfortable lunch in a chop and then I raised sail and anchor without recourse to the engine. In Hawke Anchorage the No. 2 jib was replaced by the genoa which Ian Oliver had delivered to the boat that morning. The wind became SW2 and it was a leisurely sail past Immingham on the spring flood.

Here I remember another last sail on 29 September 1959 (my log goes back to 1957). In the 18-foot Sandmartin centre-board sloop and my new wellies from the Co-op which I still have, I sailed from Stone Creek with Steve Drewery, then in his seventies. He was a Patrington Haven character in charge of sluicing the Haven drain with its mud dredger or sludge boat specially designed by Steve's father and so effective that, when it rotted, they could do no better than build an exact replica. Steve taught me to beware of the lower Humber in a strong westerly, still good advice today, but on that occasion there was a gentle north-easterly. We landed at South Killingholme and walked along the bank to the memorial to the Pilgrim Fathers.

Is South Killingholme Creek still navigable I wonder? It is now land-locked behind the upstream arm of the Immingham jetties. It used to be called Sam Flatman's Creek: he had a little white cottage there with an off-licence for ale and porter sold from the door.

My return to Hull was rewarded with a marvellous sunset – blood red behind the Humber Bridge.

In contrast, the first sail of the season is accompanied by an anxiety and lack of confidence engendered by weeks ashore. This year mine was on 31 March, the day after launching, and the high pressure 1040 millibars showed in mist and light winds.

In the lock with *Cracker* was *Morning Rose II*. I asked Dave Peacock if he was going back to Brough. 'No, just a shakedown cruise.' It sounded a rather grand description of a trip on the river but I soon knew what he meant when I realised that I had made fast my mooring line without passing it behind the lock wire strop.

Thereafter *Cracker* drifted gently about the river whilst I cleaned the coal dust and winter's grime off the decks and cockpit.

Does a late finish and an early start presage a good season's sailing? By the time you read this you will know for yourselves.

Cracker *in Hull Marina.*

# The Log of the Doctors' Sons

*(I end, as I began, with something from my mother, Muriel Fouracre: a poem which sums up so well the joy of sailing.)*

The Skipper and his valiant crew
Sailed fast in wind and sun
And soon the miles behind them sped,
Their voyage well begun.

And here and there they tacked awhile
Or sailed the river free,
And here they stopped for fish and chips,
And here they paused for tea.

And soon fair Derwent's waters mix
With Humber and with Ouse.
And Wharfe slips down from distant hills -
Which taste do swimmers choose?

And if some danger looms ahead
Or floating logs can harm,
Is it the valiant cabin boy
Who sounds the first alarm?

And as this crew of Doctors' sons
Speeds fast to York's firm shore,
Another Doctor's family
Has weclome warm in store.